HAVE YOU
TO FINANCIAL ALIENS?

YOUR PRACTICAL GUIDE TO TRANSLATING THE COMPLEX FINANCIAL UNIVERSE TO PROTECT YOUR PORTFOLIO FROM BEING ZAPPED BY SHRINK RAYS!

A hard-hitting, much needed book!

by Coach Pete is about the current confusion between the financial world and consumers, and how relevant topics could be more clearly discussed.

In this book, thirteen of the top planners in the nation discuss topics using easy to understand language, giving the reader a "behind the scenes view" of the inner workings of the financial world.

Have You Been Talking to Financial Aliens?

Your Practical Guide to Translating the
Complex Financial Universe to
Protect Your Portfolio From Being
Zapped by Shrink Rays!

Peter J. D'Arruda
Investment Advisor & Radio Show Host

AUTHOR: Peter J. D'Arruda, Investment Advisor
and Radio Show Host

CONTRIBUTING WRITERS: Jerry Clark
Bob Grace
Lee Hyder
Joel Johnson
Jeff Knoedl
Bryan Philpott
John Pollock
Mike Reese
Peter Richon
Eric Scott
Christopher Sleight
Bill Smith
Brad Zucker

LAYOUT : H. Donald Kroitzsh

Published by:
Financial Safari Press
1135 Kildaire Farm Road
Suite 200
Cary, North Carolina 27512

Telephone: (919) 657-4201
Website: www.FinancialSafari.com
Email: Pete@FinancialSafari.com

Prepared by:
Five Corners Press
Plymouth, Vermont 05056

Printed and bound in the United States of America

Have You Been Talking to Financial Aliens?

ISBN: 978-0-9777993-3-6 $19.⁹⁵

DEDICATION

I would like to thank my wife, Kimberley, for her hours of help in editing and organizing. Without her help this book would have only been a collection of ideas. With her help, this book has become a financial user's manual. A how-to book that should be consulted each year and any time a sudden change of income strikes a household.

I would also like to thank the thirteen planners who contributed to this book.

My daughter Caroline (Carrie) also needs to be mentioned as there were a couple of times that Mommy and Daddy couldn't play hide-and-seek because we were busy discussing and arranging this book.

CONTENTS

FOREWORD

"You are always only one choice
away from changing your life"

— Marcy Blochowiak

How many times have you made a financial decision only to realize later that you neglected key evidence that was right in front of you? Why didn't you see it? Were you bound by your own experiences, a prior way of doing things, a preconceived notion of the way things are? Worse yet, how many times have you made a financial decision knowing only half of the story or listening to someone who had no expertise? Or did you not understand some information because you were talking to an "alien" about your finances who used language and terminology you did not understand?

This is not unusual. It is totally human. From time to time, we all find that the way we see the world is limited by unconscious notions of what we believe reality is. But there is a contrasting conscious choice we can make: the choice to live in a state of financial discovery. In translation.

You should not be afraid of the financial world simply because you do not understand the jargon advisors and others in the financial world use. Often time, people in the financial world sound like aliens because the words they are using make no sense.

The financial "translation," a type of financial discovery, this book provides will expand your possibilities for the future. With a new financial understanding, you can revisit old assumptions in order to expand your financial ideas for the future. At the end of this book you should rethink your financial strategies in light of your financial goals. Are they in line? Do you need to make any changes in light of your new-found understanding of the financial world?

To get started on the path of financial understanding, we will talk to experienced financial advisors, also known as the "Financial Alien Translators Who Assist, Lecture, Learn, Educate and Train team" (FAT WALLET team), from across the country. This FAT WALLET team will give you an insider look into the financial world and translate the complicated financial world into something that is easy to understand, relatively speaking! Hopefully this translation will help you make more informed choices as you put together your own financial roadmap to meet your own financial goals.

First, let's meet the FAT WALLET team that is going to be translating for us:

> **Jerry Clark** – 15 years of experience from Ridgewood, New Jersey.

> **Peter D'Arruda**, RFC and Radio Show Host – 18 years experience from Cary, North Carolina.

Bob Grace, JD and RFC – 41 years of experience from Fort Meyers, Florida.

Lee Hyder – 20 years of experience from Akron, Ohio.

Joel Johnson – 18 years of experience from Wethersfield, Connecticut.

Jeff Knoedl – 12 years of experience from Little Rock, Arkansas.

Bryan Philpott – 8 years of experience from Charlotte, North Carolina.

John Pollock – 21 years of experience in the financial world from Allen, Texas.

Mike Reese, CFP™ – 15 years of experience from Traverse City, Michigan.

Peter Richon – 4 years experience from Raleigh, North Carolina.

Eric L. Scott – 28 years of experience from St. George, Utah.

Christopher Sleight – 20 years of experience from Sarasota, Florida.

Bill Smith, RFC – 16 years of experience from Sandusky, Ohio.

Brad Zucker – 25 years of experience from Las Vegas, Nevada.

I asked these advisors to be a part of the **FAT WALLET** team and to answer a set of questions that often confuse people. Each chapter in this book represents a different question posed to the **FAT WALLET** team. The easy to understand answers follow. At the end, you will have a complete guide to understanding your personal financial situation and goals for the future. There is no need to talk to any more financial aliens.

The **FAT WALLET** team translated twenty-two important financial issues that are very important to understanding your financial reality. However, so as not to cause more confusion by having too much information in one book, which might give the aliens another chance to wreak havoc, I decided to turn this into a Financial Trilogy. This is a must have for everyone's bookshelf. Keep your eyes open for parts two and three.

Sit back and enjoy the ride as the **FAT WALLET** team translates the alien financial jargon into something useful for everyone. Let us be your guides through the Financial Universe and it's alien language.

— Coach Pete

CHAPTER 1

*"It is tempting, if the only tool
you have is a hammer, to treat
everything as if it were a nail."*

— Abraham Maslow

What kind of potential client do you feel you can best help?

Chemistry, as it relates to working with your advisor, is very important. How do you know if you are working with the right advisor? The answer to this question will be different for each individual person. Do you want an advisor who explains everything he/she is doing only after listening to exactly what you want and backs it up in writing? Or, are you happy just looking at your balance every couple of years? Do you want an advisor who is a gambler or one who is conservative? Do you have an accumulation or distribution planner? Do you even know the difference?

Our **FAT WALLET** team had varied answers to this question, proving that it truly is an individualized decision for the advisors and the potential clients. However, there was a common theme among the answers – advisors want to help those that want to be helped, have an open mind, and want to hear about financial options that meet their needs based on their stage in life.

Joel Johnson – I can "best help someone who cares about other people ... and appreciates value in the form of good advice and counsel. "

Eric Scott – "My heart tells me that I want to help everyone but there are some people you just cannot help and others do not want your help. Because I cannot help everyone, I feel I am on a journey to help those with a desire to live their retirement years to the fullest. I want to help those who wish to control how much they pay in taxes, how much they want to protect their retirement assets from losses and those that do not want to outlive their income. I have found that these are usually middle-class people."

Mike Reese – I am "best suited to work with someone retired, or nearby, who is conservative and requires 5% or less income from their portfolio. They recognize that their biggest risk is losing money in their portfolio. If they do not go backwards, they will be fine."

Bryan Philpott – "I love to work with clients who have an open mind and truly care about the financial security of their retirement and their family."

Bill Smith – Potential clients "must want my help. I cannot help someone with their finances if they are not willing to accept my help. They must want to have their money safe. I cannot sit down with someone and help plan for someone's retirement if they want all their money at risk. Lastly, we can help those who need guaranteed income they cannot out-live."

Jeff Knoedl – I can "best help someone who wants to improve their net worth without increasing their market risk."

Bob Grace – I like "clients who truly understand what safety is and are looking for only safe places to invest their money in retirement - people who are open-minded to new concepts, willing to investigate new ideas, and develop a trusting relationship with their advisor."

Peter Richon – His short and sweet answer to the type of person he likes to work with is "one that would like to be helped. (You can lead a horse to water…)"

Lee Hyder – I can help someone who, "first and foremost … [has] an open mind. A mind is like a parachute, if it's not open all the way it's just not going to work.

> We all suffer from: 'We don't know what we don't know,' but sadly enough we do not know what it is we do not know till it's too late. That is a mouthful. My job is to explore what it is a potential client wants to accomplish with their financial retirement plan, determine what they are currently doing and be sure that what they are doing will take them where they want to go, and if not then I must make some suggestions to help get them back on track."

Brad Zucker – The "potential clients [I] can best help are those people who cannot afford to lose their life savings, gamble with their money, or take big risks, because they are retired and will not go back to work to replace long-term losses."

Christopher Sleight – My "ideal client is one who is in the final phase of their work career or is ready to retire. I believe that the biggest disconnect in our industry is that people do not change their investment philosophy from working to retirement. When you are working and earning a paycheck you can afford to take on more risk in your retirement accounts but when you retire and give up that paycheck, your portfolio needs to change from accumulation to preservation and income-driven investing. It is no longer about what you make; it is now about what you keep that will lend to a financially secure retirement."

John Pollock – I look "to work with clients I like (this may seem a small thing but it isn't), and the most important attribute is a client that listens, or in other words is coachable. I have found in the years that I have been working with clients that the worst decisions made by my clients are those based on emotion. If I facilitate or enable their hysteria I will eventually be blamed for the bad decision, so if I am going to be blamed for bad decisions I want them to be solely mine. My approach is to be very disciplined and have steadfast guidelines so I am less likely to make bad decisions."

TRANSLATION — **Financial advisors can provide financial advice and can be a valuable source of information. However, the answers from our FAT WALLET team show that the client needs to enter the relationship with an advisor knowing their own** financial goals and what they want to accomplish. Also understanding risk, the client's own tolerance for risk, and the facts about risk given the client's stage in life are very important.

Clients need to let their financial advisor know the client's financial goals so the financial advisor can provide financial advice that will meet these goals. If the advisor does not listen to the client's goals, or makes recommendations that do not take into account the client's goals, then it might be time to look for a new advisor.

CHAPTER 2

"The road to success is dotted with
many tempting parking spaces."

— Will Rogers

What are your three FAVORITE asset classes?

Generally, picking asset classes is tricky and time consuming. There are all kinds of asset classes – from a high risk asset class to a fixed return class and everything in between. All financial advisors,

consultants, planners, and salespeople should be familiar with all of these assets classes, but often they will have a favorite asset class they recommend to their clients. You can tell a lot about an advisor by what they consider their favorite.

"Core & Explore" Retirement Portfolio Planning

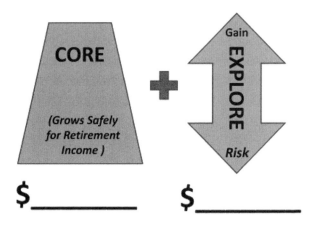

© 2010 CoachPeteRadio.com

Joel Johnson – "My three favorite asset classes are guaranteed insured income products, real estate, and high dividend-paying equities."

John Pollock – "This is a tough one because I NEVER buy based on the 'hot' asset class. I do not make choices like this. There are too many uncontrollable unknowns. I prefer to control what can be controlled. Anyone that is predicting the future is foolish, it cannot be done regardless how slick the charts and graphs, or how smart someone says they are, it just cannot be done with any consistency (anyone, however, can get lucky, but luck is not an investment strategy).

I choose to focus on narrowing down the types of investments. Investments designed to grow in value and investments that generate income. Picking the best in each category eliminates the need to analyze every product in the market place. For example, where does a CD fall, growth or income? It cannot grow in value other than the reinvestment of its income so it is an income vehicle. Now that we have established that, can we find something with the same amount of risk that does a better job than a CD in producing income? Can we find something that is more tax efficient in generating income? The answer is unequivocally yes to both questions. This is why you should never own a CD. I can control my risk choice, I can control income producing choice, and I can control my tax efficiency choice. I CANNOT control or predict the future.

Here's another example of how I can use this simple litmus test with a 'hot asset class.' GOLD! So does gold grow or generate an income? The real answer is neither. It does not pay interest or dividends. Some would argue that it grows because of the last few years. Measuring the entire success of an asset class based on a few years is a bad idea that keeps repeating itself (tulip bulbs hundreds of years ago to tech stocks, housing prices recently). What about looming inflation? Gold is a hedge, right? NO! Look up the definition of hedge, gold is far more volatile than inflation. Gold only grows in value if it is speculated up, not through actual growth like a company stock would and does.

Bottom line: Picking asset classes is just a version of gambling that I steer my clients away from."

Mike Reese – My "three favorite asset classes are hybrids (fixed index annuities being a good example), long-term stock options (both puts and calls), and commodities."

Bill Smith – I like "Fixed Income, Large Cap Value and Cash."

Bryan Philpott – I like "taxable ETF's, Index Annuities, and Tax Free ETF's." (Quick translation – He likes taxable exchange traded funds, or mutual funds, Index Annuities, and tax-free mutual funds).

Bob Grace – My "three favorite asset classes are safety, safety, and safety. There are only three safe places for money. One is a bank, FDIC insured. Number two is government bonds, backed by the full faith and credit of the United States government. And, finally, fixed annuities, including indexed annuities, which I consider to be the safest and have the best opportunity. There's nothing else out there that is not affected by interest rates, market environment, or speculation. Therefore, 'safety' means guaranteeing that when you wake up tomorrow morning you have at the very least what you started with the night before."

Brad Zucker – My "three favorite asset classes include mutual funds, variable annuities, [and] annuity accounts."

Jeff Knoedl – My "favorite asset classes are Fixed Index Annuities, Exchange Traded Funds (ETF's or mutual funds) and Life Insurance."

Lee Hyder – I have three favorites, "not in any order of preference:

1. I love life insurance, yes, life insurance. If that statement has not made you close the book and turn on the TV, good for you. No other asset class can offer so many of the benefits of life insurance. No other asset class, I believe, has been so misunderstood and underutilized. First, you know exactly the cost of the policy. Normally it will never go up but can be reduced. You know the exact amount of the benefit. You may not know the date of the check but you know exactly how much it will be for. Can you make that same claim with your 401k? NO! Did I mention the benefit is 100% tax free? Did I also mention you can use it to create future tax-free income to help fund your retirement on a free basis? Don't get me started on life insurance because I will never quit singing its praises. How about

using it to pay for an after death Roth conversion for a spouse and having the insurance company paying up to 70% of the tax for you on the Roth conversion!

2. I am also a big fan of Fixed Index Annuities for people that are not comfortable with market risk and need more safety, predictability, and guarantees than you can find in the stock market on a day-to-day basis. When you add an income rider to a Fixed Index Annuity you have a great combination. You have a product that can not only guarantee your principal from loss and limited upside potential, you also get the ability to create a guaranteed predictable income you and your spouse cannot outlive.

3. This is not as much of an investment class as it is an investment strategy or style. I am not a big fan of mutual funds. They may be easy to invest in, and they do not require a large amount of money to open them or contribute to on a ongoing basis, and they have done a great job for many people over the years, but they are not the most tax efficient investment and can have a lot of expenses and fees associated with them. Many of these fees are not as transparent as they should be, giving the investor a false sense of what they really cost to own. With mutual funds you need to look at

Administrative fees, Management fees, 12b-1 fees, loads, transaction expenses and Taxes. With that being said, I like to work with separate accounts because they offer direct access to institutional money managers, are more tax efficient, offer lower trading costs, and have a lot of customization and flexibility."

TRANSLATION — As expected, our FAT WALLET team's favorite asset classes vary. However, there were several common concepts among their answers to keep in mind with considering the best asset classes for clients: safety, tax considerations, and diversification. These are important concepts for people to understand when considering any type of investment strategy:

• As a client, do you want more safety in your investments, or do you want more risk? Your answer may depend on your stage in your investing life – are you just entering the work force in your 20s or are you nearing or in retirement?

• Do you want the most tax advantaged investments? Are you considering the tax advantages of investments now or in the future?

• There is more on diversification in Chapter 3, but are you diversified in your investments on a risk scale but also on a scale that considers immediate versus Long-Term needs?

The variety of answers to this question highlights the importance of clients understanding their own advisor's philosophy and making sure that matches the client's own goals. Not everyone is the same, so what will work for one person will not necessarily be right for another person. When there is a match between the advisor and the client, everyone feels good about the relationship and the investment decisions that are made.

CHAPTER 3

*"The ultimate goal isn't to win once, but
rather to win over and over again."*

— Coach Pete

What does TRUE DIVERSIFICATION mean to you and how do you explain this to your clients?

Wealth creation, protection, and distribution are the purposes of diversification, as well as the value of true diversification.

Wealth creation is a function of maximizing cash flow and prioritizing its application to desired outcomes within targeted time frames. At the same time, it is important to create awareness of, and strategic responses to, the most probable risks to those planned outcomes. Many mistakenly believe this means how much should be invested in what funds for how long to get rich. NONSENSE!!

Tax reduction, benefit elections, debt management, risk premiums, estate documentation, adequate cash reserves, lifestyle expense budgeting, and household budgeting are ALL more important than whether you are in a cheap or expensive fund or, as you might hear from some advisors, what your efficient horizon, optimization point, and Monte Carlo probability calculations might be. "Financial diversification" is about establishing base lines and future progress points which require annual check-ups to verify and quantify wealth creation. It is not a short-term project, it is a lifetime process.

Your choice of the right financial professional is not a simple one, but can be important in our goal of achieving true diversification. It could also be the most significant investment decision you will make in your lifetime.

The main objective of this topic is to help provide you financial security today and far into the future. Your financial planner should provide an in-depth evaluation of your financial profile in order to create a structured plan based on saving, investing, and true diversification. Your financial goals will always dictate which financial instruments and diversification profile best suit your needs. Diversification is implemented in order to increase the probability to obtain financial success. A true financial planner will help you maximize your financial efforts with a well-organized diversification plan and continue to provide you details and recommendations throughout your relationship.

Brad Zucker – "[T]rue diversification means having the adequate six months of cash reserves to cover monthly expenses, enough money in safe money accounts that will not risk principal, and the balance in potential growth with risk."

Jerry Clark – "A person is truly diversified when they have their monies allocated across all sectors in the free market system. The true calling comes when people have their monies allocated across these sectors with the right weighting to meet their specific needs. This means that there are no better asset classes than another. All are important and should be invested in."

When Jerry explains the process to clients he angles the conversation towards how people should not and cannot speculate with their money. It is his opinion that a properly balanced portfolio that is rebalanced throughout the year and meets the clients' needs allows the clients to stay invested and remove fear from the unknown.

Jerry believes strongly that most people are taking on too much risk in their portfolios than what they are comfortable with. They are in few sectors and they tend to lean towards high risk because they have not been properly trained in risk management.

John Pollock – John is concerned because "diversity in a portfolio is one of those things that is simple to explain but difficult to achieve." He came up with the Diversity Trinity to help with this. "The trinity requires you be IN something, WITHIN the thing your IN, and OUTSIDE of the thing you are IN and WITHIN." He uses a simple example. You are IN stock. Do not own just one stock, but be WITHIN stock (he targets 12,000 to 14,000 stocks in 20+ countries; how he does this is for another time). Then, once this is done, you need to be OUTSIDE stock completely, even better would be something that has no correlation to stock at all (this means bonds are out).

John says he has not had a single portfolio come into his office that does not violate this simple rule. He has added to this rule to help clarify it over time. One of the guidelines is keep any single alternative strategy to less than 10%. (So if you insist on gold, keep it under 10% and diversify in coins, gold jewelry companies, gold mining etc.)

Like he said, "simple but not easy."

Lee Hyder – "Diversification means not having all your eggs in one basket. Not having a portfolio with investment overlap. It is easy to have many different mutual funds but many people do not realize even with different funds you may be investing in very similar investment classes within these different funds and that eliminates the apparent diversification."

Bob Grace – "Diversification during your working years, what I call 'paycheck years', are a number of acronyms and abbreviations: Large Cap, Small Cap, REIT's (real estate investment trusts), value funds (a type of mutual fund), etc. All of these acronyms and abbreviations do not really mean anything other than risk. Diversification in retirement is very simple, risk or safety. There is no in-between. There is no such thing as just a little risk. It is like saying you're just a little bit pregnant."

Eric Scott – I like "to approach diversification in two ways - risk and liquidity.

First, since I work with those who are either retired or close to retirement, I feel I have a responsibility to ensure that my clients have enough money for their primary needs and then I look at their risk tolerance. Diversification is based on the needs of our client and can be between bonds, CDs, stocks, mutual funds, money markets and annuities. Based on their risk tolerance, I determine which of these investments would be best for the client's individual circumstance.

Second, liquidity for diversification is based on short-term, medium-term and long-term money and needs. Short-term is based on the needs from one month to a year. Medium-term is based on the needs from one year to five years. Long-term is based on any needs longer than five years that plays a part on what investments we use."

Mike Reese – "True diversification means a true mixture of asset classes. For example, one cannot be truly diversified by holding several types of mutual funds only, as no mutual fund can provide guaranteed safety. True diversification comes when you have a base level of guaranteed investments like CDs, government bonds, or fixed annuities combined with non-guaranteed elements like stocks or mutual funds."

Joel Johnson – "True diversification means that we have flexibility year after year to decide where we take income from without depending on the equity markets to go up in order for a financial plan to work. Of course, this means spreading investments over different asset classes such as stocks, bonds, real estate and hard assets such as commodities and guaranteed Treasury or insurance products."

Bill Smith – "I explain [diversification] to my clients using the 'Rule of 100' age rule in safe accounts, which is that depending on your age, you should have a certain amount of safe vs. risk money. I also explain the fixed income annuities as well as the difference in risk" when discussing how to properly allocate a client's portfolio.

Jeff Knoedl – Diversification to me means "making sure my clients can sleep at night. It is amazing how much an investor can lose and then tell me their broker told them they were 'diversified.' I explain to them that there is a big difference between 'low risk' and 'no risk'" when it comes to diversifying a portfolio with risky investments and safe investments.

Peter Richon – "Diversity means difference. You want a difference in your investment types. You do not want all of your portfolio in real estate, you do not want it all in gold, you do not want your portfolio all in cash, you do not it want all in stocks, bonds, mutual funds, annuities, the lottery, or on one poker hand in Vegas. If you are 'all in' in any situation or asset class it could be disastrous. But some of each is great. I would never go 'all in' unless it is on a sure thing and not much is a sure thing in this world."

Christopher Sleight – "True diversification for retirees is different. We may want to utilize bonds which could mean corporate bonds or municipal bonds. We may want to use the family of fixed annuities. We may want to throw some public, non-traded REITs (real estate investment trusts) in there and possibly, depending on the client's assets, risk tolerance, and income needs, we may want to sprinkle a few preferred stocks in for a little market exposure if it pays a nice dividend while we hope for a positive market return."

Bryan Philpott – "True diversification means completely keeping your safe money in a totally different account than your risk money."

TRANSLATION — There is not much debate among the FAT WALLET team in what diversification means. "Diversification" means having assets in a variety of investment or financial vehicles. Determining what those financial vehicles are must be determined by the client and their advisor based on the client's goals and needs.

Clients should also make sure they completely understand the financial vehicles used to create a diversified portfolio that their advisor is recommending. For example, if a broker recommends mutual funds, the client needs to ask and investigate whether the stocks within the mutual funds differ enough to provide diversification. If not, analyze different funds or look for other options besides mutual funds.

The client should also inquire about risk, fees and expenses associated with the recommended diversification vehicles. Are there hidden fees and expenses that will automatically reduce the client's account? If the client wants a safe investment, does the recommended diversification vehicle provide safety or is it actually an investment associated with risk?

With full and complete information about investment alternatives, clients and advisors can make sure the client will achieve actual diversification across the classes of investments while factoring in the short, middle and long range goals of the client.

CHAPTER 4

"The future isn't what it used to be"
— Yogi Berra

When do you recommend someone buy life insurance?

(In what situations do you feel it is an invaluable addition to an overall financial plan?)

There are many cases where life insurance makes sense, regardless of whether the person is using it for retirement planning or for estate planning. Despite the myths and misconceptions that exist today, the fact remains, if set up properly and for the right reasons, life insurance is one of the only financial vehicles where one can turn pennies into tax-free dollars at death and get a guaranteed return on their investment.

There are so many great uses of life insurance. It will be interesting to see what the **FAT WALLET** team has to say.

Bryan Philpott – I recommend people buy life insurance "when they hate paying taxes and they have loved ones they care about. The only situation where we find life insurance to not be of great value is when someone just does not have a source of funds to pay for it or there are no heirs or charities they support."

Christopher Sleight – "Life Insurance is tricky…for some clients it is an emotional purchase ('I want to leave a tax-free legacy to the kids') and for other clients it may be used to replace an income stream for a surviving spouse. Example: A husband chose a larger pension payment but when he dies the pension goes with him creating a significant loss of income upon his passing away. In situations like this, life insurance can give the surviving spouse a lump sum payment she can then reinvest to generate the income she lost when her husband passed away.

I will also use life insurance as a more clinical tool to leverage tax-free monies for my higher net worth clients. Used this way, life insurance can help alleviate estate tax issues that the heirs may have upon settling estates that are vulnerable to estate tax."

Jeff Knoedl – Life insurance is good for clients that "have a need to leave their loved ones debt-free, to pay estate taxes, to leave tax-free money, to pay taxes on IRAs, or to replace an older policy with one that gives the client more protection or reduces their premium or both."

Bill Smith – "If you love someone or owe someone, you should always have life insurance. You do not want to leave your loved ones to bear the cost of your death."

Joel Johnson – "There are three reasons I recommend people buy life insurance:

A. To finance an obligation or liability to someone or something such as debt, taxes or a buyout of a business.

B. If the person loves someone or something and wants to guarantee a promise.

C. Using high cash value, general account based life insurance to create a tax-free, inflation proof stream of income."

Mike Reese – "Life insurance is appropriate ANY TIME you want to provide financial security to a loved one after your death. For example, a widow could receive no better account from her deceased husband than the tax-free death benefit of a life insurance contract. You need to remember that taxes increase for surviving spouses due to filing single vs. married on the income tax return. Thus, receiving a tax-free benefit is huge for that person.

Further, every dollar that is intended for charity should be a life insurance dollar. Why would you give a charity $1 at your death when you can instead give that $1 to an insurance company which would then give your charity $3 or $4?"

Eric Scott – "We recommend life insurance after our 3-step review process (tax planning, income planning and risk profile/management planning) to those who have a high sum of taxes to pay. These taxes can be generated from estate taxes, large IRAs, 401(k)s, 403(b)s and other financial sources.

Next, if there was a substantial loss of income, which would make a difference to the lifestyle of the spouse left behind, life insurance is important. We also look at their portfolio to see if there are substantial losses that they would want to restore so they can pass that money on as a legacy to their heirs.

Every client's situation and needs are different so we approach each visit a little differently."

Bob Grace – "When clients are trying to pass assets on to their heirs or the next generation, life insurance is the most efficient instrument to do that. When I say efficient I mean in both potential return and tax efficiency. Life insurance is a dollar bill for future delivery at a discount treated on the most favorable basis of any asset in the entire Internal Revenue Code. Life insurance is invaluable to a financial plan when a client absolutely wants to pass some assets on to the next generation and wants to assure it is done at a discount, meaning you cannot live long enough to put 100 cents into the dollar that will be passed to your heirs, and you want to absolutely ascertain that that money is available to your heirs when you pass on."

Lee Hyder – "Boy did you ask the right guy a life insurance question. Where to begin? Life insurance is important for these reasons:

- It allows you to leave a predictable tax-free amount of money to your spouse to live on after you die: This avoids what most people do, which is to make their spouse the beneficiary of their traditional accounts, such as their IRA or 401k. Being the beneficiary to a 401k and or IRA is not a bad thing but why pass them a tax liability when you can pass them a tax-free distribution?

- It allows you to plan for a predictable financial loss: When you die your pension for your spouse is reduced and your spouse loses all her Social Security benefits. Life insurance helps make up that loss.

- It is a guaranteed way to make up all that money you lost in the stock market.

- It allows you to diversify your portfolio and use the power of leverage: I know of no other financial vehicle that can create so much wealth, tax-free, with such small amounts of premium."

John Pollock – "Life insurance is thorny because it is a very lucrative industry, but just because someone makes money selling it does not mean it is bad. (Vegetables are sold at a profit and my mom said these are good!) But something that pays very well can and does get abused. Here are some guidelines.

1) When young, buy term and buy enough to pay off all debt, replace your income and send your kids to college, if you were to die.

2) Do not buy life insurance as an investment, UNLESS the cost of the insurance is substantially less than the taxes you are and will be paying (this strategy is reserved for the wealthy during accumulation years so applies to very few).

3) Ignore the advice in 1 and 2 when you are estate planning. If you are in jeopardy of having to pay massive estate taxes, then life insurance will become your ally. But, drive down the cost of the insurance

(survivorship polices) and make sure proceeds are outside your estate (ILIT's – Irrevocable Life Insurance Trusts). Basically you are choosing the lesser of two evils because, when estate planning, you are choosing between paying premiums to the insurance company while alive or paying massive taxes at death to the government. If you do nothing it defaults to the government."

Jerry Clark – "Until this year I have neglected life insurance in my business. That was until hearing advisors talk about the transfer of wealth going tax-free to families. I go down the life insurance path when I hear people saying they are not intending on using their IRAs in their lifetime. We then help them to redirect the assets towards life insurance to leave more of the IRA tax-free to the family than taxable."

Brad Zucker – "Life insurance is recommended for large estates that may be subject to a federal estate tax. It is also recommended for replacement income due to loss of pension and Social Security at the death of a spouse."

TRANSLATION — **There is a general consensus among the FAT WALLET team. Life insurance is a great vehicle to pass money to your heirs or a favorite charity** tax-free. It is also a good way to replace income that is lost by the death of one spouse.

The new use of life insurance as a "back up" for Long-Term care insurance is also rapidly gaining traction inside the financial world. (There is more on Long-Term care insurance in Chapter 6.)

On the issue of whether life insurance should be used as an investment or a way to diversify your portfolio, our FAT WALLET team was not in agreement. This is another area where it is important for an individual to meet with a trusted financial advisor to review their financial situation and determine whether making an investment in life insurance is appropriate for them.

CHAPTER 5

"Life can only be understood backwards;
but it must be lived forward."

— Kierkegaaed

In what circumstances would a ROTH conversion make sense for a client?

If there was a way for you to pay taxes on your money today and then have it build tax-free into the future, giving you a tax-free income in retirement, would you put money into it? There is, it is called the ROTH IRA.

The ROTH is not a type of investment vehicle; rather, within a ROTH, you can select from thousands of different investment and savings vehicles. The ROTH is a strategy and should be considered in all financial plans. Just because it should be considered, however, does not mean it is a good fit in all cases. This is why people should talk to their

The Four Buckets

| Taxable | Tax-Deferred | Tax-Free | Tax-Free X 2 |

advisor about the advantages and disadvantages of a ROTH for them.

A competent advisor should be able to explain the advantages but also any disadvantages of starting a ROTH or converting a current IRA or 401(k) into a ROTH account. The advisor should also be uniquely familiar with how to act on this process if it does make financial sense in the client's situation.

Let's see what the **FAT WALLET** team feels about the ROTH.

Brad Zucker – "ROTH conversions are recommended for a client who wants to reduce future income taxes, lower the amount of taxes on Social Security income, reduce forced required distributions they may not need, and provide their heirs with a lifetime of income tax-free wealth."

Jerry Clark – "ROTH conversions only make sense when the client is young enough or is not in need of the assets. We do mostly 'ROTH carve outs' rather than full conversions. People are content to see some of their monies being converted and growing tax-free and limiting what they pay to the government."

John Pollock – "If you do not need the money then [a ROTH conversion] is an excellent idea and will be a gift that gives into the next generation. Here are some guidelines to the conversion:

- Target 6% or higher returns, which will help shorten the breakeven time when paying the upfront tax.

- Pay the tax with money outside of the IRA, which preserves that tax advantages of the ROTH, and takes some taxable money off the table at the same time.

- Consider other IRA conversion strategies; they may actually serve you better than a lump sum ROTH conversion.

- Consider converting over time to reduce your over all taxes and soften the tax hit.

The most important guideline is do not convert just because you can. One idea is not a plan, just like one pair of pants does not make a wardrobe. Consider the conversion as a part of your overall strategy and make sure the pants fit in the wardrobe you already have."

Lee Hyder – "When a client is very concerned about the future tax liability they will have to pay on IRA distributions, a ROTH conversion conversation would be very important to have. However, if they do not have funds outside the IRA to pay the tax I may advise against the conversion. If they are such a conservative investor that there is not much likelihood to make back the tax they paid for the conversion in the first place I would also not recommend it. For many people it is just too expensive and really does not make sense. There are great calculators available on line that can help you determine if a ROTH may or may not work for you."

Bob Grace – "The ROTH conversion makes sense when the tax liability does not affect cash flow or the income needs of the client. If the client believes the tax rates are going to go up it is better to pay tax at a lower current rate than to pay a larger tax at a larger rate of tax in the future. However, the client must have enough cash outside the conversion to pay for the current tax liability. If converting to a ROTH is going to affect the lifestyle or cash flow of the client I would not recommend it be done."

Eric Scott – "ROTH conversions are based on tax planning, income planning, and age. We look at each case individually to determine whether this particular conversion makes sense or not. If the client will be in a better tax situation for their retirement years and have more useable income with the conversion, we would show them the potential tax savings over their lifetime and how using this tax law is to their advantage. We are always very careful to look at income, tax brackets, and their needs to make sure they are making an informed and sound decision. We have found that the ROTH conversion, for the right client, can save hundreds of thousands of dollars in taxes as well as provide tax-free growth, income, and inheritance."

Mike Reese – "ROTH conversions make the most sense when all three of the following components are in place: younger age (65 or younger), high tax bracket (25% federal and above), and when the account is being reinvested."

Joel Johnson – "I would recommend a ROTH conversion to a client if they want to control future taxes or disinherit the IRS."

Bill Smith – "I would recommend a ROTH conversion when you can pay the taxes without using your IRA money, if you want tax-free future income and/or if you don't plan on spending the money during your lifetime. You will want to make sure you have at least 5-6 years to re-coup the taxes. It may also be viable for a tax-free, stretch ROTH IRA."

Jeff Knoedl – A ROTH conversion is advantageous "if a client wants to reduce or eliminate tax on their Social Security or is concerned about future tax increases. One of the best times to convert is when the taxable account has decreased in value."

Peter Richon – "If you feel that you may be paying lower taxes now than what you could possibly be paying in the future, it is the right time to consider a ROTH."

Christopher Sleight – "ROTH conversions are another tricky subject because on the surface they look great but they do not work for everyone. I believe that the younger you are, the better the idea of a ROTH conversion is. We, as advisors, must always remember this: How long will it take to earn back what was paid in taxes as a result of the ROTH IRA conversion. In volatile times like this, where interest rates are incredibly low, it could take 3-5 years just to break even on the taxes before the benefits of the tax-free income from the ROTH IRA can be beneficial."

Bryan Philpott – ROTH conversions are appropriate "after a complete tax analysis is done and [the client] will be able to recover the tax damage in 2-3 years. We also advise people that it just does not make sense for everyone."

TRANSLATION — Well, you can ask a simple question but sometimes the answer is not so simple. ROTH conversions, as our FAT WALLET team seems to agree, can be beneficial. They allow people to pay tax now, hopefully at a lower tax rate, and enjoy their IRA account later on tax-free. However, whether a ROTH conversion is appropriate for any particular person must be thoroughly analyzed. The age of the person contemplating a ROTH conversion is important as is the thought that taxes are going up in the future.

Moreover, because taxes must be paid at the time of the ROTH conversion, there is a significant current tax liability to consider. The FAT WALLET team generally would only recommend the ROTH conversion if the person can pay the tax liability with money outside of the IRA and if the money used to pay the taxes can be recovered within two to three years.

Because of the intricacies of a ROTH conversion, someone should only consider such a conversion after a thorough review and understanding of the benefits and consequences.

CHAPTER 6

"Excuses are the nails used to build a house of failure."
— Don Wilder

What do you tell someone who is 55⁺ who has not considered purchasing Long-Term Care insurance?

I believe that everyone should have some type of Long-Term care insurance (LTCI) as there are two certainties in life:

1. We are living longer as a society, and

2. It gets more expensive each year for long-term care.

There are three ways to pay for long-term care coverage:

1. Self-insure - Use money you save to pay for care. The risk is that you could go through your whole estate with an extended stay and what if both you and your spouse both need care?

2. Pay monthly premiums for LTCI – You must make sure you get the proper policy and be aware of the

"use it or lose it" mentality that exists with some LTCI policies.

3. Buy a life insurance policy or annuity with a Long-Term care rider – Such a policy keeps you in control of your principal (no more "use it or lose it"), while giving you two to five times the amount you put into the policy in the event of a Long-Term care need. The problem is you have to have a lump sum of money to participate.

Generally, my thoughts on LTCI have been that if husband and wife had enough money to provide for both of their potential long-term care expenses, they were really not insuring each other but rather their estate. In that  case, if there was a budget for insurance premiums, life insurance may be a better purchase. On the other hand, for small and medium size estates, LTCI does protect against the possibility that the care of the first spouse will wipe out the estate leaving the surviving spouse in bad shape.

In the past, the biggest complaint about LTCI was the obvious risk that you will spend a lot of money in premiums and never need the care. However, you can think of it like your car insurance or your homeowners' insurance, etc. - you are insuring against a risk and hope you never need it.

Recently, though, I learned of a new long-term care solution that I really like because it just makes sense. As someone who expected it to be "too good to be true," I thought I would find lots of problems when I started looking at the details. But that is not the case. The more I looked at the details, the more I liked it.

It is essentially a combination of life insurance and Long-Term care insurance. Depending on the amount and the terms, if you need long-term care, the insurance company will pay for your care. The amount the insurance company pays you for the long-term care is then subtracted from your death benefit of the life insurance. If you never need the long-term care, your life insurance death benefit will stay intact. This seems like a win-win situation.

Now let's look at the FAT WALLET team's thoughts on Long-Term care insurance.

Bryan Philpott – "We inform people that 1 out of 2 seniors will need assisted living care. Why do they want their assets at risk of Medicaid spend down?"

Christopher Sleight – "Long-Term care insurance, in my opinion, is another emotional sale. If it allows my clients to sleep better at night and they can buy it at a young enough age then I'm all for it. There are a number of 'Discovery

Questions' to ask when considering selling Long-Term care insurance to a client such as:

Where did your parents, grandparents, aunts and uncles spend the last 2 years of their lives?

Does Alzheimer's run in the family?

Do you have a genealogic history of long-term care needs (stroke, Alzheimer's disease, etc.)?"

Peter Richon – "Long-Term care insurance is something that should be considered very seriously. Nothing can lay ruin to a well made financial plan quicker than unforeseen medical expenses, especially ones that require long-term or continuing care."

Jeff Knoedl – Before recommending Long-Term care insurance, "I find out how important it is to the client to make sure they are not going to be a burden to their heirs. It can be compared to living in your house with no homeowners insurance. You might save a little money each year, but what if ...?"

Bill Smith – "I recommend that clients consider the costs and look at all of their options, including the cost of doing nothing. Sometimes in those scenarios, doing nothing at all will cost more in the long run."

Joel Johnson – "I would tell someone 55 + that has not considered buying Long-Term care insurance that they have three choices:

A. They can self-insure and keep the risk of paying for long-term care and then pay dollar for dollar out of assets/income if the need arises.

B. They can buy insurance thus shifting the unknown risk to an insurance company for a known premium.

C. They can create legal entities such as trusts and limited partnerships, whereby giving up control of an asset; however, the asset is protected and the client can potentially qualify for Title 19/Medicaid."

Mike Reese – "I share with my clients that, as prudent people, they have no choice other than to at least investigate their options. Legitimate options include Long-Term care insurance, life insurance with Long-Term care riders, or self-insurance. The key point is that the risk is analyzed and addressed with open eyes."

Eric Scott – "Purchasing Long-Term care insurance goes back to needs and risk. Studies show that 1 in 2 people over the age of 65 will spend some time in a nursing home. We like to get our clients' feelings and experiences on the subject first. We then look at their income and total assets.

I like to ask them this question: 'If you happen to be the one that goes into a nursing home how is it going to be paid for?' There are only four options (for people without Long-Term care insurance):

1) Your money will cover the costs until it runs out;

2) The government will cover the costs until they run out of money, and, seeing as benefits are often cut to save money, that door may close sooner than we think;

3) Your children will cover the costs until their money runs out; and

4) You take out a reverse mortgage on your home (the reason I mention this option is because it may be the only way your spouse has enough income to live on).

The alternative of having to depend on any of those four options, of course, is to look at purchasing Long-Term care insurance to protect your assets and money. We help people look at the risk and how they can take care of it.

We also educate them on Long-Term care insurance because there are so many options in providing this. Traditionally you pay and, just like homeowners insurance, if needed the insurance company will pay. Another option is depositing money into an insurance account that offers to build cash value, has Long-Term care and a tax-free death benefit with the ability to cancel and always get your money back. You can also use annuities with tax-deferred interest growth, but include a Long-Term care feature within that annuity.

Times are constantly changing and we have found that most people are not being educated about all the options available to them. We believe sharing those options with them allows them to make an educated decision instead of sticking their head in the sand like an ostrich and hoping not to face it."

Bob Grace – "The biggest exposure of our society today is not dying too soon but living too long. The average cost currently of a one-year stay in a nursing home is about $70,000 per year. The average stay that is publicized on the radio and television is two and a half to three years, including rehabilitation stays in nursing homes of people who have just come out of a hospital and cannot afford to remain in the hospital. If you eliminate those rehabilitation stays, the average senior with dementia or Alzheimer's stays in a nursing home about eight years. That can devastate even a wealthy family. If you do not transfer the liability, 100% of it is going to be on your shoulders, unlike what most people do with any other risk which is to transfer it to a professional insurance carrier."

Lee Hyder – For people that chose not to buy Long-Term care insurance, "I hope they have a lot of money set aside, because by default they have chosen to self-insure. I know it can be expensive, but today there are a lot of options and choices when making this decision. I would ask clients not wanting Long-Term care insurance to reconsider and to explore all the newest options they may not have seen in the past. They may be unaware that there are even policies today that will refund, at the person's death, 100% of the premiums to their beneficiaries if they have not used the policy."

John Pollock – "Long-Term care is a product most often purchased by those that do not need it (they can self-insure) and not owned by those that need it the most (they will run out of money quickly and then go directly to Medicaid).

For those that can self-insure it is a financial preservation tool, it protects their assets against spend down for Medicaid purposes. For those that cannot self-insure, it is a life and body preservation tool. Do you really want the government 'taking care' of you?

Armed with these facts, the decision is easy to make for most people."

Brad Zucker – People considering whether or not to purchase Long-Term care insurance must understand "the alternatives to traditional Long-Term care insurance, and that if they do not own insurance, they must have an alternative plan."

TRANSLATION — The bottom line - ask your financial advisor about Long-Term care insurance and whether it is right for you. It could be that someone is able to self-insure their long-term care needs. It could also be that someone's family history may indicate a more certain need to consider long-term care alternatives.

It is not a requirement to have Long-Term care insurance, but it can make someone's final years less stressful to themselves and their family. However, as the FAT WALLET team mentioned, there are all types of long-term care options for people and consulting a financial advisor is very important.

Long-Term care insurance has changed dramatically over the years since its inception and now offers options of a return of the premiums if long-term care is not eventually needed. In this way, it acts much like a savings vehicle.

Eventual nursing home care needs are too large of a potential liability not to even consider investing in some type of plan to combat that potential expense. Everyone should, at the very least, begin a discussion with their family and their financial advisor about their long-term care needs and whether their financial plan accounts for potential long-term care expenses.

One thing is for certain, ignoring long-term care needs will not make the event any less likely to happen. Nothing can wreck havoc on someone's successful financial planning than an uncovered, extended long-term care stay.

CHAPTER 7

*"The key to success in life is using the
good thoughts of wise people."*

— Leo Tolstoy

Are you familiar with the "Investment Rule of 100"?

If so, how close do you follow that rule for your clients?

The Rule of 100 does not apply as a firm investing rule, but is great when used as a starting point in building a financial plan. Quite simply, you take 100 and subtract your age. The number left is the amount of your portfolio you should expose to risk.

An example, assume a 65 year old, 100-65 = 35. Thirty five percent of this person's portfolio could be exposed to risk. The other sixty five percent needs to be in a secure financial vehicle.

It is important to note that investing and investments are not one size fits all. People can vary in different ways, including:

- current net worth,
- investing goals,
- investing purposes,
- investing time frames,
- risk levels,
- knowledge,
- experience, and
- values.

Because of these differences, I believe the Rule of 100 is a good starting place from which to make investing decisions.

Will the **FAT WALLET** team agree with me? Let's find out.

Brad Zucker – "We use the 'investment Rule of 100' to determine how much of a client's money should be safe and how much should be at risk."

Jerry Clark – "I use the Rule of 100 all the time as a starting point in asset allocation. We always show clients the Rule and how they are probably taking on more risk at their age than they need to.

However, I take the Rule one step farther. When a 70 year old can take on 30% risk with their assets I break the 30% down using the Rule of 100 again. Spreading the risk 70% in bonds and 30% in stocks from the original 30% allocated to risk. This is an over the top conservative approach; however, the client really never sees their portfolio move with giant swings."

John Pollock – "I am familiar with the Rule of 100 but often times splitting up assets between fixed and equity based on your age minus 100 is too simplistic. Some are advocating changing the rule to the 'Rule of 115' due to increased life expectancies, but this does not solve the overly simplistic strategy. What about tax bracket? What about distributions from non-qualified vs. qualified? What if this is still too risky? What if this is not risky enough?

I focus my clients on values, vision, and goals then strategies, tactics, and products so there is little room in this formula for a simple number like the Rule of 100 dictates."

Lee Hyder – "The Rule of 100 is a vital part of the first conversation I have with any new client. Like all rules it does not need to be followed to the letter but it is a good place to start to determine if my client is too heavily allocated in the market vs. safer asset classes. The Rule is a great guide to determine how someone is allocated when we first meet and give them some new ways at looking at new allocation percentages to different asset classes that may offer more safety that are more in alignment with the Rule of 100."

Bob Grace – "I am very familiar with the Rule. It indicates if you are 70 years old, 70% of your assets should be in safe places and 30% in growth and opportunity. So I tell a client if they are willing to lose 30% of their money that is not a bad rule to follow. I also suggest they should not be subjecting any of their money to loss and therefore 100% of their money should be in a safe place that has the opportunity, if the market performs, to grow. That would be fixed indexed annuity."

Eric Scott – "I use the Rule of 100 to help my clients understand just how much money they should have at risk. In my presentations I give people a tape measure that extends to 100 inches. I ask them to pull the tape measure out until it reaches their current age and we talk about their investment experience and then we place one hand at their current age and we stretch the tape measure all the way out to their life expectancy, though their life may be shorter or longer than that. When they see the difference between their hands, I ask them this question: 'How much risk do you want to take?' This is important because when they see how long they have lived and just how soon they could pass on, many of them begin to think about risk differently for the first time. If the client is 70 years old, I explain to them that they should only look at taking risk on 30% of their money based on the study that shows that 1 out of every 2 people is now living into their 90s. We want to make sure that that money lasts."

Mike Reese – "Yes. I use the Rule as a baseline starting point with all of my clients to begin building their perfect retirement portfolio. I am perfectly willing to vary off of the result of the rule either more conservatively or more aggressively based on a client's circumstances and feelings regarding risk."

Bill Smith – "I follow the Rule of 100 to a 'T'. The only exception to that is if the client we are working with would like more safe money than the rule provides. You cannot have enough 'safe' money."

Jeff Knoedl – "I am familiar with Rule of 100 and follow it closely. Most of my clients want most if not all of their retirement assets protected from market volatility. The Rule of 100 helps me illustrate how most have too much risk exposure in the stock market. There is a myth that the more risk you take the greater the reward."

Peter Richon – "100% of investments are risk-based. Savings are the monies that are meant to be kept safe. It is important to understand the difference. The Rule of 100 says take your age and subtract it from 100. The number you have remaining is the MAXIUM percentage of your assets that should be kept at-risk. (Example: for a 65 year old the equation would be 100-65 = 35% at risk).

However, in these volatile market conditions, depending on the risk tolerance of the client, some people might want to divide this number by two: (100-age)/2 = maximum at-risk amount (using the example above: (100-65)/2 = 17.5% at risk), especially if they are within the Financial Red Zone (when you are in or within five years of retirement, recently divorced, widowed, disabled, or had a sudden change in income).

Christopher Sleight – "The Rule of 100 is a fundamental roadmap for determining risk tolerance for retirees. I believe in even more preservation-minded investing during these times of extreme volatility and economic unrest.

Once you lose principle it can NEVER make interest for you again. I always lean towards the conservative side with my retired clients."

Bryan Philpott – "Yes, we follow the Rule of 100 to the tee. If someone is 65, then 65% of their assets need to be in safe accounts where they have no chance of losing money. We inform clients and individuals that this is the only way to win the retirement phase. They can only afford to risk 35% of their money if they are 65 because dollar cost averaging and time just are not on their side."

TRANSLATION — The FAT WALLET team generally agrees with me. The Rule of 100 is a useful guide to use when considering how much of someone's money should be at risk. It is useful because it takes into account the time younger people have to make up any money lost by allowing for more money at risk, and also takes into account the reduction in time to make back money lost as people age.

However, knowing the Rule of 100 cannot replace the advice of a financial coach. A financial coach and Investment Advisor is in a position to talk to someone about any factors that may make fluctuation from the Rule a wise decision – whether it is fluctuation to even less risk because of the market conditions or fluctuation to slightly more risk if the person's financial position can support that risk. Thus, people should discuss the Rule of 100 with their financial professional to determine what is best for them and their financial position.

CHAPTER 8

"True discovery consists not in finding new landscapes but in seeing the same landscapes with new eyes."

— Marcel Proust

What do you tell someone who is looking for lifetime income using the assets they have?

As we age, more and more of our funds need to not only be in safe places, but also in places that guarantee a lifetime income. This is called "income planning." An income plan, also known as a "Basket Strategy," can help ease people's worries about retirement income as well as market volatility.

The basic theory of a "Basket Strategy" is to separate your money into 4 places, or baskets, each one with a specific purpose. One basket provides immediate income and three others grow to provide income down the road. At least one basket should be guaranteed income you cannot outlive, with the remaining assets passing to children, grandchildren, or charity.

The main goal of a "Basket Strategy" is to provide a 15-year income stream from three baskets, and at the

end of that 15-year period, the final basket still contains an income account with a value equal to or greater than the total amount used to start the "Basket Strategy." The final basket is always built with a guaranteed income withdrawal benefit to take the account holder the rest of the way. This helps establish a predictable and guaranteed yearly income.

Income planning is unique and must be customized for each person depending on their risk tolerance, needs, and time frame in which the income is needed.

The **FAT WALLET** team also answered the same question:

Brad Zucker – "Like all of our clients, we are in agreement that future inflation will rise faster than the rate it has in the last ten years. Thus, it is important to have an income plan in place."

John Pollock – "I try to ascertain if where they want to be (the amount of monthly income they want), and where they are (current assets, plus retirement income streams) times the erosion of inflation (we use the hundred year average and a double digit calculation) is actually attainable.

If not, we try to determine if they need to save more, get better returns, spend less, or work longer.

If they do have enough we use some strategies and tactics that minimize risk and maximize returns, these tools will help them hit their goals and protect them from making bad decisions which would undermine their own stated objectives."

Lee Hyder – "I would have to ask these questions first: "What are the current investments they plan to take lifetime income from? Are these investments in a guaranteed investment class?

I know this sounds almost childish to say but it needs to be said: You cannot guarantee income from a non-guaranteed account.

Would it surprise anyone to learn that if the portfolio you were using for monthly income went down 40% that you would have to also reduce the income that you were taking from the account or jeopardize running out of money during retirement? If you are looking for guaranteed income you first have to examine the underlying portfolio and the risk you are exposed to. For a true guaranteed retirement income, I would lean toward many of the latest products available today that have been specifically designed to create guaranteed retirement income."

Bob Grace – "There is only one asset available to provide lifetime income and that is a lifetime income benefit rider available on a fixed or variable annuity. The value of acquiring a fixed annuity is that the asset base is more likely to grow than a variable asset base. Also, the fees for income riders on fixed annuities are much less and the compound growth rate is much greater than on almost every variable annuity. A lifetime income benefit rider will absolutely guarantee that you can never ever run out of money, even if you live to 100, 110 or 120."

Eric Scott – I like to ask a very important question of those who visit with me: 'What is more important to you if you happen to live to 100? Your money or the income that currently comes from that money?' I always hear that it is a trick question, but it is not. Based on what may happen in the future with interest rates, the market, taxes and inflation, if all you did was hope your money lasted, you could run out of money and income. After explaining that, I ask again: 'Is it your money or income that is most important to you?' Most people understand what I am asking then and answer 'income.' We then share with them ways to guarantee their income for the rest of their lives, have control of their money and even if it runs out they will not lose the income."

Mike Reese – To have lifetime income from the assets a person already has, those assets "absolutely, positively MUST be guaranteed. Their retirement income should not be affected based on what the stock market does or does not do."

Joel Johnson – "If someone is looking for life-time income using the assets they have, I would tell them that the only institutions that can guarantee lifetime income are the government and insurance companies. If clients are comfortable moving away from guaranteed safety and income, then we will discuss preferred stocks, investment grade corporate bonds, real estate investment trusts and alternative investments such as gas and oil programs or equipment and leasing. The latter can be structured with a very high degree of safety but not an absolute guarantee. Returns on these alternative investments can be 6% - 12% or more."

Bill Smith – I would tell people looking for lifetime income that they must "**never** risk the money they need to provide lifetime income, the necessities in life, or the money they need to be able to go out and enjoy life. You should never, ever risk that money."

Jeff Knoedl – "I tell my clients there is a way to receive a guaranteed income for life without losing control of the asset.

Also, I mention that all plans are not the same. I see too many situations where someone's current financial person gave very bad advice about a supposed income plan. A few months ago, I met a prospective client who told me her broker did not disclose that she was required to wait 10 years to begin the income payout. How is that an income plan when the nice lady was in need of immediate income? The only immediate aspect of this was the commission the broker earned!"

Peter Richon – "Trying to maximize your guaranteed lifetime income can be a tender and emotional subject. People must be realistic. If you are used to living on $40,000 of after tax income per year and want to retire at the age of 62 with a retirement nest egg of $200,000 in your 401k or IRA, how long will you expect that to last?

If you are looking to guarantee a lifetime income then you must have your money positioned where it can provide a consistent amount for however long you may live. For example, in a guaranteed income plan, 5%

of $200,000 would produce $10,000 per year for however long the person lives.

However, in income plans that are not guaranteed, fluctuations in account values due to market forces can affect their income dramatically if they plan to utilize a certain percentage of their assets each year. In the previous example, if the market drops the value of your account to $160,000, taking the same percentage will only net $8,000 in income. Also, for qualified accounts you must factor in taxes."

Christopher Sleight – "I believe that if we can guarantee an income that will meet or exceed the income needs while still leaving a level of liquidity within their portfolios, it's something we must examine. No one likes 'locking up' their money but it beats the heck out of losing your life savings and having to go back to work at 70 years of age. My goal is always to give my clients choices- as long as those choices follow the investment philosophy for retirees: Preservation and Income needs first."

Bryan Philpott – "We run a cash flow analysis first by finding out how much money they need from their investments after Social Security is taken out of expenses. Then we look to see what rate of return they will need to achieve. If they are taking more than 5% of their retirement funds they are in survival zone. They may want to consider some type of annuity to guarantee an income stream."

TRANSLATION — We are all historians when it comes to the stock market. However, past performance can never guarantee future results. The last decade has taught us how fragile our money can be if not in the proper financial vehicle. Proper income strategies help in establishing peace of mind as well as minimizing the risk of loss of retirement funds.

Let's picture a water wheel. The first basket in the wheel is pouring out water (income). While the first basket is pouring out income, more baskets are filling up, preparing to pour water (income) once the first basket empties. This example shows the constant motion involved in income planning so there is a consistent and predictable cash flow with no worries about account evaporation.

Because everyone is different, however, it is important to have a financial coach problem-solve with you in order to help build, preserve, and transfer wealth, with the goal having all the money you need, when you need it.

CONCLUSION

The **FAT WALLET** team has provided lots of useful information in an effort to clear up some of the confusion in the financial sector. Financial information often sounds like it is coming from aliens because it cannot be understood or is too generic to be helpful. Financial situations are unique to individuals so generic information spoken in alien gibberish is not useful.

Our **FAT WALLET** team's information is meant to clear up some confusion and educate people on various areas in the financial world with the hope of  giving people the base of knowledge to understand their own financial situation and their own financial needs and goals. With this base of knowledge, people can ask questions they need to ask and seek advice of qualified experts in an effort to meet their financial goals.

These are just some of the more prevalent topics that are surrounded by misunderstandings concerning financial planning, strategies, concepts, and products that the public faces today.

You have now started on the path of financial understanding, and I hope the **FAT WALLET** team's insider look into the financial world and translations of complicated financial topics has made this world a little easier to understand.

The goal of the book was to help you make better educated choices as you march down the financial field of life.

The key concept to understand is that you should not try to navigate the alien financial world without a competent advisor and coach, not when there is a local **FAT WALLET** team member just a phone call or office visit away.

Now get out there and **fatten that wallet!**

FAT WALLET
TEAM BIOS

JERRY CLARK — RIDGEWOOD, NEW JERSEY

 Founder and Principal of RJL Financial Group, Gerard (Jerry) Clark, has helped the residents of New Jersey successfully retire and stay retired for more than a decade. He believes that with proper planning, you should be able to maintain the lifestyle of your working years in retirement but also, in many cases, elevate your lifestyle for the golden years.

In 1998, Jerry established RJL Financial Group with the goal of changing the way people look at retirement planning. He wants to motivate and enable pre-retirees and retirees to achieve predictable retirement savings results—giving them the ability to feel secure about their retirement future.

Prior to starting his own personal practice, Jerry worked on the New York COMEX and for a large insurance services provider. He is a registered life and health insurance professional, as well as an investment advisor representative and holds the series 6, 63 and 65 securities licenses.

Jerry is also a former professional golfer and played in various tours nationwide. He still enjoys playing golf with his clients, friends and family in his spare time.

Jerry and his wife Lisa have been married more than 15 years and have two daughters, Riley and Josie, for whom RJL Financial Group is named. Jerry participates in the annual Ridgewood, Somerville and Hawes Elementary School's Dad's Night, an evening where fathers come together to write and perform skits and songs in an effort to raise money for the schools.

When Jerry isn't spending time with his family, working or golfing, he also enjoys training for and competing in the annual Ironman Triathlon and has done so since 2000.

Peter J. D'Arruda, RFC® —
Cary, North Carolina

Financial coach and guru, Peter J. "Coach Pete" D'Arruda is the founder and president of Capital Financial Advisory Group, LLC. Mr. D'Arruda is also founder of "COACH PETE'S FINANCIAL SAFARI"™ radio show heard throughout the United States. Coach Pete specializes in investment, income, retirement, and estate planning and has developed a process he calls "Financial Insulation" to keep retirement assets in a safety bunker and prevent financial evaporation of assets due to unexpected market declines.

Coach Pete loves the look on a client's face when they realize they really do understand the retirement planning process instead of being blindly lead down the path by a financial salesman.

Coach Pete is a Registered Financial Consultant (RFC®) with the International Association of Registered Financial Consultants, as well as an Investment Advisor Representative. He is a voluntary member of the National Ethics Bureau as well as the Better Business Bureau. He enjoys being interviewed by many national and local tv and radio networks as well as the local and national print media. His article on "Basket Planning" as it relates to lifetime income strategies remains a favorite among advisors who call his office seemingly each month.

He resides in the Cary, North Carolina with his wife Kimberley and their one and only daughter Caroline.

BOB GRACE, JD, CLU, ChFC

Robert E. Grace, a Juris Doctor (JD), is a Chartered Life Underwriter (CLU) and a Chartered Financial Consultant (ChFC), with over forty years of experience providing estate, retirement, and tax planning for individuals. He has been trained by, and become a member of, nationally acclaimed financial expert, ED SLOTT's "Elite IRA Advisor®" group. Bob's training and experience place him among our country's leading financial experts.

Bob was a practicing estate planning attorney in the State of Ohio where he specialized in family wealth transfer and tax planning. He expanded his experience working with brokers' clients in two of the nation's major national financial corporations.

In his current practice at Grace Tax Advisory Group, LLC, Bob and his team help individuals and business clients establish sophisticated – yet easy to understand – solutions for protecting and preserving wealth while minimizing tax exposure.

Fort Myers News-Press readers named Grace Tax Advisory Group, LLC "*Best Income & Retirement*

Planners" in both 2008 and 2009, in the annual Best of Southwest Florida poll.

Bob and his wife, Rose, enjoy an active Florida lifestyle as year-round Fort Myers residents. They spend quality time golfing and yachting. Bob is an active member of the Cape Coral Power Squadron and committed to safety on the water.

Lee Hyder, CSA — Cleveland, Ohio

Lee is the father of two great children, Codi, who is also in the financial services industry in the banking community, and Jessi, who is in the health and fitness industry in New York. Lee is married to Lizzi, the love of his life and his true soul mate who he credits for creating a home life that has afforded him the opportunity to serve so many families of Northeast Ohio for over 19 years. Lee has helped countless families create the picture perfect retirement we all dream about having. One where you know, really know you will never run out of money during retirement. Retirement income with high taxation is like a car with no fuel. It's just not going to get you where you want to go. With that in mind Lee believes in helping pre-retirees create a retirement plan that includes some form of tax-free income. Lee is the author of the book "Estate Planning for Everyone" which can be down loaded free of charge from his website, and Lee has been seen on local Cleveland TV, heard on the radio coast to coast and been quoted in numerous newspaper and magazine articles. Lee is a sought after public speaker on retirement topics and issues facing pre-retirees and retirees alike. Lee's battle cry has always been "Your financial future deserves a 2nd opinion." In today's complicated world it's no longer to okay to live by "what you don't know won't hurt you!" What you don't know about your portfolio, taxes, and fees can rob you and your family of that special retirement you once hoped to have and enjoy. Lee lives in Akron, Ohio.

JOEL JOHNSON, CERTIFIED FINANCIAL PLANNER® — CONNECTICUT

Joel Johnson has been in the financial services industry for over 18 years. Among his many personal accomplishments, Joel has devoted his time to many causes which positively affect the lives of others. He served two years as a missionary in both the Philippines and Canada. He also spent six years working for Young Americans Showcase, an organization which visits many countries and teaches young adults the importance of staying in school and making healthy life choices.

Joel has been a Connecticut resident and active member of the Connecticut community for nearly 21 years. The following are some of the organizations that Joel has served or is serving as financial advisor or board member:

- Active Member and Finance Committee Member, Trinity Covenant Church, Manchester

- Financial Advisor to the Children's Home of Cromwell, a not-for-profit organization that houses, cares for, and educates youth at risk

- Board Member, Boone Biblical Ministries, a not-for-profit religious radio station in Des Moines, Iowa

Joel and his wife Wendy have been married for 22 years. They have four sons, whose ages range from 10 to 20 years of age. As an adult volunteer, Joel is active with his sons in the Boys Brigade, Little League, and Pioneer Boys.

JEFF KNOEDL, RFC® — LITTLE ROCK, ARKANSAS

Jeff is President and Founder of Knoedl Retirement Advisors, LLC, a company dedicated to serving and educating pre-retirees and retirees. Jeff began his career in financial services in 1996 and his focus is working with individuals in developing retirement, income, and tax minimization strategies for all sizes of estates. He has helped hundreds of clients reduce unnecessary income, social security, and estate taxes while at the same time increasing spendable income.

He is an Investment Advisor Representative of Knoedl Retirement Advisors, LLC a Registered Investment Advisor. Also, he is a Registered Financial Consultant (RFC®). He is a public speaker and can often be heard on local radio stations. Jeff is a member in good standing with the National Ethics Bureau and accredited member of the AR Better Business Bureau.

BRYAN PHILPOTT, RFC® —
CHARLOTTE, NORTH CAROLINA

Bryan Philpott is a Registered Financial Consultant, which is presented to Financial Advisors who meet 7 criteria related to Education, Examination, Experience, Ethics, Financial Licensure, Conduct, and Continuing Professional Education.

Bryan has been engaged in financial services since 2003 and is the President and Financial Advisor of the firm Aspire Wealth Management.

JOHN POLLOCK — DALLAS, TEXAS

John Pollock, is the President of John Pollock, Inc. and Pollock Advisory Group, Inc. John began his career on the corporate side of financial services working with CFO's of major corporations helping them to manage cash flow and account receivables more effectively and cost efficiently. His extensive corporate background gives him a unique perspective and valuable experience not typically found in the financial services industry.

John's goal is to help clients develop and implement a plan designed to build and preserve a life and legacy of meaning. His passion for his work is articulated as author of two books: *Legacy Planning* and *The Nest Egg Cookbook*. John has enjoyed being the featured speaker for hundreds of audiences conveying his unique concepts such as Segmenting, Financial Gravity, Diversity Trinity and Timeless Wisdom, Strategic Application. These time-tested and consistently effective concepts are the culmination of past business experience and years of helping clients.

Mike Reese — Traverse City, Michigan

Michael Reese, CFP®, CLU, ChFC is the founder and principal of Centennial Wealth Advisory based in Traverse City, MI. He is a Certified Financial Planner®, Chartered Financial Consultant, and a Chartered Life Underwriter. He has been cited in numerous industry publications for his expertise on retirement planning, including "US News & World Reports."

Mr. Reese specializes in creating innovative tax and investment solutions to help his clients "Live Well" during their retirement years. This may include significant tax reduction on retirement plans, leaving more money available for his client's enjoyment. Or it could mean portfolio optimization techniques that guarantee your principal while simultaneously maximizing growth opportunities. Additionally, it might include income optimization strategies, which guarantees your income while keeping your tax liability to a minimum.

In addition to his financial advisory practice in Traverse City, he also assists other financial advisors throughout the country by being the featured educator at Advisor's Excel's "IRA College" in Topeka, KS.

At the "IRA College", Mr. Reese teaches top financial advisors throughout the country a number of tax planning strategies that he uses to significantly reduce the taxation on his client's retirement plans.

He's also a featured speaker at multiple industry events. If you live in Michael's local area, you can see Mr. Reese on NBC's Money Matters every second and fourth Monday of each month at 6:25 AM with Melissa Smith. Or listen to his 5-Star Retirement Radio talk show every Saturday morning from 8-9 am on 106.7 YOU FM.

Mr. Reese lives in Traverse City, MI with his wife Becky and 5 children.

Peter Richon — Raleigh, North Carolina

Peter is a graduate of the University of North Carolina at Chapel Hill. While there he majored in Communications and received a degree in Media Studies and Production with a minor in History. He quickly went on to Chief Producer then Program Director/ Operation Manager for four of the top news and talk radio stations heard throughout Research Triangle Park and Raleigh, North Carolina. He also assisted the launch of several Internet radio stations including StateGovernmentRadio.com which focused on and documented the day to day operations of North Carolina's State Government. Through his time in radio he interviewed countless professionals, personalities, politicians. He began hosting and producing talk programs centered on financial education in 2003. Since this time Peter has interviewed some of the top professionals in the financial industry, learning various approaches to financial planning, marketing, and the "behind the scenes" operations of financial firms. Peter went on to assist in the national syndication of The Financial Safari™ which he still hosts and moderates to this day. He is also a licensed insurance agent. In 2009 Peter and his wife Amber celebrated the birth of their son Braxten.

Eric Scott — St. George, Utah

Eric L. Scott is the President of Eric Scott Financial. He has been serving people since 1983 by helping them reduce taxes, increase their income, protect their assets and live their retirement years to the fullest. When you sit down with Eric, you'll find that he sincerely cares about your concerns and desires and will listen to you with undivided attention.

Eric loves spending time with his family and is active in both his church and his community. He and his wife, Sherri, live in St. George. They have 3 children: Paul, Katie and Ryan. They also have 3 grandchildren: Lexi, Calvin and Oriana.

CHRISTOPHER SLEIGHT — SARASOTA, FLORIDA

Managing Director of Global Capital Private Capital. For years, Mr. Sleight has worked with clients specializing in preservation of principal and managing the most important time of their lives. He recognizes that people are searching for a reconnection in their financial relationships and he offers a vehicle to forming that personal rapport with the company's professional staff.

Prior to joining Global's team, Mr. Sleight was a compliance officer for Florida's Department of Business and Professional Regulation. He made the transition into the financial planning industry to serve a community in need of a professional understanding of their legacy of wealth.

Mr. Sleight along with his wife and two daughters, reside in Sarasota, Florida where they are members of Incarnation Christian Church. He enjoys playing tennis and coaching his daughters' soccer teams.

BILL SMITH, RFC® — SANDUSKY, OHIO

Retirement expert, William "Bill" Smith is the founder and president of Great Lakes Retirement Group, Northern Ohio's premier financial planning firm. Bill specializes in investment, retirement, and estate planning and has made it his personal mission to educate and assist Northern Ohio's pre-retirees and retirees on how to properly plan for a secure retirement.

Before founding Great Lakes Retirement Group, Bill worked as a financial planner for a corporate financial firm. He quickly realized he could only help his clients in a limited capacity. Corporate restrictions prevented him from performing comprehensive account planning services, as well as restricted his time with each client. He has been working independently to better serve his clients since 2000.

Bill is a Registered Financial Consultant (RFC®) with the International Association of Registered Financial Consultants, as well as an Investment Advisor Representative. He is a voluntary member of the National Ethics Bureau as well as the Better Business Bureau. He is often sought after for his financial expertise by local news channels in Ohio including CBS Channel 19, ABC News Channel 5 out of Cleveland and CBS Channel 11 out of Toledo. He has also been interviewed by the Wall Street Journal, Smart Money Magazine, TheStreet.com and Senior Market Advisor.

He resides in the Cleveland area with his wife Erica and their three children, Hallee, Blake and Cameron.

Brad Zucker — Las Vegas, Nevada

Brad Zucker, Financial Consultant and President of Safe Money Advisors, Inc., has been helping seniors to reduce taxes and keep their money safe since 1986. Brad is a proud member of the Better Business Bureau, Clark County Dept. of Business and Licensing, Las Vegas Chamber of Commerce, National Ethics Bureau, National Association of Insurance and Financial Advisors, and is registered with FINRA (Financial Industry Regulatory Authority).

NOTES